WITHIN

AND

BETWEEN

Poems by

Robert H. Deluty

GATEWAY PRESS, INC.
Baltimore, MD   2000

Please direct all correspondence and book orders to:
Robert H. Deluty
4783 Ilkley Moor Lane
Ellicott City, Maryland 21043

Library of Congress Control Number 00-92613
ISBN 0-9704201-1-0

Published by
Gateway Press, Inc.
1001 N. Calvert Street
Baltimore, MD 21202

Printed in the United States of America

To
Barbara, Laura, and David

Table of Contents

at cliff's edge
board meeting
talent show

67 Senryu:
sunshine breaks through
approaching the bar
elderly waiter
Nobel winner's death
all night
fourth-grade cellist
next morning

68 Senryu:
blind woman's home
taxidermist's sign
rainy summer night
their car a hits a deer
satellite dishes
asked how it's going
old fans reminisce

69 Haiku/Senryu:
calorie-conscious
three-year-old's ears
at the pharmacy
girlfriend's parents
trees on fire
grade-school trombonist
hand-me-down shirt

70 Senryu:
murderer's neighbors
TV interview
debutante walks in
estranged mother
in the OR
the five-year-old cries
wolf-whistler

Lessons

He loved to tell the story of how,
On his first day of Yeshiva
In Poland's Jewish Ghetto,
Mothers brought honey cakes,
Shaped like the letters of the
Hebrew alphabet,
So that their children
Would come to associate
Learning with sweetness.

A brilliant man, deprived by war
Of even a high school education,
He set foot on a college campus
More than fifty years later to attend
His first son's Ph.D. conferral.
When introduced to the faculty,
With utmost respect and pleasure,
He bowed.

His second son, now a professor,
Remembers these stories
As he teaches his daughter
Her ABCs.

Perfectionist

Anxious when working,
Guilty if shirking.
Fearing heightened expectations
When work is commendable,
Dreading disapproving gazes
For efforts lamentable.
And should perfection be achieved,
Comfort is painfully brief,
For a fall from grace is awaited,
Stifling hope of lasting relief.

Wedding Dance

The bride and groom sit in the
Center of concentric circles.
Surrounding them, hand-in-hand,
Dance the major players in their lives:
Boyhood pals, college roommates.
First cousins, new friends.
Uncles, teachers, colleagues.
Siblings, grandparents, mother, father.
Threads from different eras and places
Woven together for a few minutes,
Forming a set of familial, communal
Identity bracelets.

Line Art

She, 7, he, 3, and five friends
Take turns sprawling across the
Driveway, tracing each others'
Perimeters with sidewalk chalk.
Hours later, passersby stop and
Stare at what appears to be a
Crime scene involving the murder
Of the seven dwarfs.

Halloween at Children's Hospital

On the psychiatric wards, it was
More joyous than Christmas,
More treasured than birthdays.
Cookies, candy corn, cupcakes,
Masks, black crepe, skeletons.
A chance to be someone/something else:
The incest victim, a pampered princess;
The terrified boy, a bloodthirsty ghoul;
The psychotic girl, a quiet lake.
A time for receiving without guilt,
For converting true horrors
Into imagined, festive ones.

Entitlement

Entitled
  To rage because of insult
  To hate because of mistreatment
  To steal because of deprivation
  To destroy and be destroyed.

Or

Ennobled
  With a single, precious entitlement,
  One's birthright as a human being:
  To be respected.

77290

  I remember his left arm.
  Leather-tough, lightly freckled,
  Thick as a fireplace log.
  Culminating in short, dense fingers
  With near-perfectly round nails.
  Most memorable, though, was the forearm,
  Damaged by five blue numbers:
  His concentration camp tattoo.
  A daily/nightly reminder of
  Evil and martyrdom,
  Faith and resilience.

Haiku/Senryu

high school commencement ...
widower saves a seat
for his late wife

•

high noon—buzzards
atop the Joe Camel billboard
pause as they refresh

•

ankle bracelet
flutters with each step—
butterfly tattoo

•

in her garage
two new cars
both by *Fisher-Price*

•

beach chair on front porch
shivers in October wind,
sheds last grain of sand

•

goes to the market
just to hear another voice—
paper or plastic

•

centenarian,
3-month-old great-granddaughter
exchange toothless smiles

A Mother's Gift

Pregnancy with you was a pleasure.
And, during your delivery, I
Actually laughed out loud—
Your feather-soft head of hair
Tickled me so as the doctor
Pulled you from me.

Such was my mother's rendition
Of the story of my birth.
Partly fact, mostly fantasy,
Largely reflecting a selfless wish
That her middle child feel welcome,
Special, loved.

Urban Escapist

Alone in his tenement home,
He avidly watches professional
Golf tournaments on television.
Not caring who is playing,
Even less who is winning,
He does not attend to the
White shoes, white faces,
Pastel pants, colorless comments.
He is riveted, though, to the
Exquisitely peaceful, pampered
Landscapes and watercourses,
Daydreaming of a life amidst
Sun-drenched acres of green, blue.

Name Calling

Recent birth announcements
Evoke a frightening epiphany:
In 60 years, most grandmas
Will be named Ashley and Tiffany.

In the Waiting Room

The older woman, blind, in her 50's,
Sat next to the one holding the baby.
The holder, 30ish, appeared distant,
Disconnected from the child.
The baby, newly awake, cooed softly.
Her tiny crushed head held
Bulging eyes spaced closer
To her ears than to her
Barely visible nose.

The blind woman was the child's mother;
The younger woman, a social worker;
The baby, one of three disfigured children
Adopted by the elder.
When asked about her children,
The mother, with a smile, noted,
They all look the same to me.
Beautiful.

Empathy

One-year-old,
Teething, miserable,
Refuses to suffer quietly.
Mother tries every trick:
Each is met with tears, tantrums.
Exhausted, hopeless,
Mother screams, then sobs.
Seeing an adult cry
For the first time,
Child quiets down,
Hands mother her bottle.

Special Delivery from Korea

Airport as maternity hospital.
Arrival gate as waiting room.
Pilot, social worker: midwives.
Baby, conceived and born
Half-a-world away, comes home
To anxious, joyous
Adoptive parents.

Therapy

A workday's depression
Evaporates as he sees
His son's handiwork in
The backseat of his car—
Gumby, with legs crossed,
Arms outstretched, seat-belted.

Saturdays

He, raised Orthodox,
Loved the teachings,
Ambivalent about the practice.
His wife, raised agnostic,
Attracted to the fellowship,
Bewildered by the rituals.
Their sons, 7 and 5,
Wanted to spend the morning
In T-shirts, jeans, sneakers.
The family compromise:
Sabbath services at
The Public Library.

Wonderland

Look at the rainbow pancake!
The little kite swims fast.
It's like a juicebox with eyes.
Dolphins are shiny as rainboots.
Children become poets
Walking through the aquarium.

Toddlersaurus

Lurching, lumbering, careening flat-footed,
Oblivious to obstacles and dangers in its path.
Hurtling head-on single-mindedly,
Arms flailing, fingers jabbing,
Mouth, tongue, and teeth primed and ready.
Wide-eyed, wild-eyed,
An admixture of delight, wonder, and purpose.
An early life form
Taking its first unassisted steps.

Balance

Old story:
—The secret to your long and happy marriage?
My wife makes all minor decisions, and
I'm responsible for all major ones.
—Minor decisions?
Like, should we buy or rent?
How should we discipline the children?
Where should we invest our savings?
Should we put Mom in a nursing home?
—And your **major** decisions?
Is there a God?
How do we achieve racial harmony?
What is the meaning of life?

Current story:
A marriage of equal partners, with each
Balancing career **and** family.
Providing child care **and** public service.
Delighting in the mysteries of God **and** of
2-year-olds.
Working to lessen strife among nations **and**
between siblings.
Seeking solace in the Great Books **and** a
spouse's caress.
Taking time to search for philosophic truths **and**
For a little girl's missing sneakers.
Striving to have it all, but
Without any delusion of achieving it.

Survivor

By his own hand, dead at 45.
For decades, his skeleton has
Rattled in the hearts
of two daughters.
The younger, now an adult,
Looks at her children, husband.
Terrified of a repetition, she
Curses genetic predispositions,
Wages war against depression,
Vows to celebrate
Her 46th birthday.

Disconnected

The near-deaf elder
Struggling mightily to hear,
The newly-verbal toddler
Groping to make desires known.
Both rageful ...
One unable to understand,
The other, to be understood.

Street Scene

Sweltering July Sunday,
Corner of Fulton and Lombard.
Husband and wife hand-in-hand
With sons aged 5 and 3
In suspendered short pants,
Black knee socks and bow ties.
With pride and grace,
They enter their church.
A Norman Rockwell family
In the charred inner city.

A Toddler's Night's Sleep

At midnight, arms are 2:45, legs 6:30;
By 1 A.M., arms gain 2 hours, legs lose 3.
Mechanical timepiece provides orderly
Backbeat to her body clock's appendages.

February/June

Whitman Sampler v.
> Three-tiered white cake.
Boxed long-stemmed dozen v.
> White-rose-and-iris bouquet.
Candle-lit supper for two v.
> Ninety gift-bearing dinner guests.
Passion v. Commitment.
Lust v. Love.
Heart v. Soul.

Laura, at 6

On the school bus
A third-grade boy told me,
You have really nice hair.
And Jake, you know, in class,
Said I have a pretty voice.
These,
Her first schoolboy compliments,
Are shared with her parents in
A heartbreaking amalgam of
Pleasure and embarrassment,
Fear and pride.

Three-Year-Old Author

Tapes two tiny papers end to end,
Folds it, scribbles on all sides.
Exclaims, "I've made a book!"
When asked to read it aloud,
Responds, "Can't. Too long."

Every Day is Halloween

At four years, he is
Part Moe "The Stooge" Howard,
Part Mighty Morphin Power Ranger.
He possesses Moe's haircut and
Negativism, his silliness and
Enlightened sense of anarchy.
Simultaneously, he is the
Newest, shortest Power Ranger.
A fearless dynamo,
Loyal and sensitive,
Innocent and bigger than life.

Better Living Through Science

With 12 million research dollars,
In the year 2008,
A team of brilliant scientists
Was able to isolate
A rogue gene that keeps kids from
Turning off bathroom lights,
Picking up their clothes, and
Avoiding sibling fights.
The scientists' efforts caused
Many family conflicts to cease,
And so they got Nobel Prizes
In both Physiology *and* Peace.

Too Long in Academia

Put latest effort in
Colleague's mailbox.
Thanks for your memo,
He noted later.
It's called a poem,
I replied.

Bertha

Romanian-born, 58 inches tall,
Fractured English, cherished family.
Obsessively neat, worried relentlessly,
Ended each good-bye with "Be careful."
When grandson went off to Buffalo,
Fretted about him alone in "Siberia."
Lived selflessly, died beloved.

Corner Store, 1966

Jet-black wigged Anna, 70,
Stood all day behind the
Counter, reading newspapers
Cover-to-cover, reluctantly
Looking up to make change,
Milkshakes or small talk.

Zig, her husband of a half-century
And dispositional opposite, greeted
Each patron with a smiling, heavily
Accented, "Nu, h'war you, pal?"
Before launching into an impromptu,
Disjointed oration on world events.

With a dime in hand, I'd visit
Anna-and-Zig's each schoolday—
To indulge in their licorice whips,
Halvah, and chocolate-covered jellies,
To escape all responsibility,
To taste sweetness, and to smile.

Father and Son

He died. He was too young
To experience retirement
And daughters-in-law;
To enjoy grandchildren
And peace of mind.

He died. I was too young
To ask him to detail his
Parents and childhood,
Dreams and disappointments;
To tell him directly that
My pride in him was surpassed
Only by my love for him.

Both too young. Now too late.

Survivor's Handball

Said he loved the game
Because the ball was like
His heart—dark, hard, small.
He'd hit each shot
At full strength, as if trying
To make the ball's blackness explode.
As if each strike
Might crack open a
Dark, hard, small heart
Forged by pain, loss.

Loan

They do their dance each workday morning.
She, in front of the counter,
He, behind, by the ovens.
They haven't spoken in months,
Not since she lent him the 5.
Before, they would exchange
Smiles, smalltalk, a wink
As she waited for the rolls
He had just baked.
On the street one June day
He approached her, whispered
Could you spare a few bucks 'til Friday?
Now, it's March.
They exchange angry glances, then
Go about their business, hoping
The other will make the move.
Return the 5! Apologize!
Be a man! she hopes.
I haven't forgotten. But now,
It's too late. Go away! he wishes.
So they continue to approach without
Contact, like flies around a flame.
Honesty's too hot to touch.

Second Born

Fewer arrival gifts,
Shorter journal entries,
Quarter as many photographs.
Yet,
No less loved,
No less treasured,
No less a miracle.

Thankless

He prays for a promotion
To the executive suite;
He gets a drunken driver
Missing him by inches.
She prays for the strength
To lose five pounds;
She gets a heartfelt letter
From a long-lost friend.
They pray for the world
To take note of their talent;
They get a day with their children
Filled with laughter and trust.

They pray for the trivial,
They get the wondrous,
Yet they ask
Why weren't our prayers answered?

Kindergarten Graduation

What could be more absurd than
Six year olds in cap and gown,
Girls in white, boys in burgundy,
Marching as one to pomp and circumstance?

Yet, nothing could be more touching.
Angelic faces, off-key voices
Singing songs of friendship and hope,
Sharing farewells with teachers, friends.

Mothers transfixed in their seats,
Alternately laughing, sighing, crying;
Fathers darting about with cameras,
Needing to wait until their film
Is developed and videos inserted
To experience their wives' joy,
Pride and sadness.

Behind a Six-toothed Smile

He'll be playing or bathing or dreaming
Or looking adoringly at his big sister
When it'll come:
A pure, heart-achingly sweet sound
Full of innocence and joy and self-satisfaction.
A sound that delights and sustains
All who hear it.
David's laugh.

Juggler

Mother, spouse, wage earner—
Roles, like juggled balls, that
Form fluid intersecting arcs.
Distance, balance, emphasis
Are relentlessly adjusted so that
None is over- or under-stressed.
Roles that must be humble,
Each willing and able
To relinquish apogee
To maintain equilibrium.

At the Market

Her five-year-old, deprived of candy,
Pitches a fit. Her four-year-old,
Similarly impoverished,
Throws a tantrum even grander.
Patrons and staff stare,
Shaking their heads in judgment.
Mom looks at children and audience,
Calmly says, "This is the last time
I baby-sit my neighbor's kids."

Answers for the Novice

Why,
Asks the weary new father,
Do people smile, laugh,
Seem downright pleased
At my being up all night
With the baby?

For some, it's simply a matter
Of misery loving company.
For others, sheer relief that
It's you and not they, or
Delight in a man bearing some
Of the child-rearing load.
For most, though, it's comparable
To taking pleasure in the
Misfortunes of the rich and celebrated:
You've been granted a miracle,
A precious new life;
So, for balance, you deserve
A modicum of annoyance.

First Day of Kindergarten

Tears fall silently
As she fills the new lunch box
Of her last-born child.

Valentines

Her face is perfectly round,
Her mother's is elegantly angular.
Yet both radiate sweetness,
Exuberance and delight.

Her eyes are dark brown almonds,
Her mother's are deep blue globes.
Yet both find joys and pleasures
That others fail to see.

Her arms are short and chubby,
Her mother's, long and willowy.
Yet both offer hugs and caresses
Of incomparable tenderness.

A Korean-born daughter,
A Long Island-reared mother,
Alike in all the important ways.

Blessed

Auschwitz survivor
Holds great-grandchild, savors
New defeat of Nazis.

Encores

The golden hits of long-forgotten tapes—
"I'll give you something to cry about"
"Why are you doing this to me?"
"This is your very last warning"—
Are reflexively retrieved
As one's children repeat
One's own classic routines.

Semantic Shifts

He smiles and offers warm hellos
And is labeled Kind.
She masters obscure facts and dates
And is deemed Brilliant.
They have their names cited
Relentlessly by the media
And are designated Great.
Single, shallow acts have
Become noble traits,
Synonymous with the
Persons possessing them.

In Hiding

She wants to cry to her teacher,
I'm terrified; instead,
She giggles nervously.

He wants to tell his wife,
I love you; instead,
He teases her playfully.

She wants to say to her parents,
I need your help; instead,
She remains silent, distant.

For, to act otherwise,
To be open, honest, direct,
Is simply too frightening.

Eraser

Had them removed
As soon as he arrived.
Before learning the language,
Buying a suit, or
Making a friend.
Viewed it as vital
To bleach the past,
To pass as American.
Instead of blue numbers, now
He had scars on a forearm
To match the scars within.

Bedtime Questions

Why don't I have grandparents?
—They died years ago.
How'd they die?
—They were killed by the Nazis.
Why?
—Because they were Jews.
What difference did that make?
—At the time, it made all the difference in the
    world.
At school, a girl said that God never gives us
more than we can handle. Didn't God give your
parents too much?
—Go to sleep. Sweet dreams.

Passover Seder

Each Spring, loved ones gather
To extol and thank God for
Miracles past and present;
To partake matzo and wine,
Salt water and bitter herbs;
To recount Israelite servitude,
Exodus and redemption; and
To rejoice in the world's
Most precious gifts:
Freedom and children.

City Playground

Rusted, netless hoops
Cast shadowed halos upon
The soaring children.

Mornings

One child rouses from sleep
With startles and ill temper,
Hits the ground whining.

The other wakens gently,
Grins gleefully, can't wait
To plunge into new adventures.

For her, at 6,
Life must be approached
Slowly, cautiously each day.

For him, at 2, each day is
Immediately embraced, cherished.
In his words: Life is goog.

Haiku/Senryu

side-by-side, carpooled
eighth grade boys, ninth grade women
sit miles, years apart

•

stalemate ...
overly polite drivers
won't stop yielding

•

pointing, laughing
as they try on wigs—
children on chemo

•

old Southern lady
punctuating each insult
with "Bless her heart"

•

eight-year-old's boyfriend
described as really cute
and a good speller

•

tortilla chip—
heading south
in a jay's beak

•

in mourning ...
his refrigerator filled
with homemade pies

Glory Days in the Bronx

It was our reward for perfect
Attendance in Hebrew School:
A day trip to Yankee Stadium.
Proudly, gleefully, we'd leave
Our public schools at noon, and
Rendezvous at the synagogue.
From there, a 3-block walk and
A 5-stop subway ride to
River Avenue and 161st Street.

Upon entering the stadium
We put on our Yankee caps,
Akin to donning our
Yarmulkes in temple.
Each of us held a
Baseball glove in one hand, a
Paper-bagged lunch in the other
(Ballpark franks, though enticing,
Alas, were not Kosher.) To us, it
Couldn't have mattered less whom
The Yanks were playing that day;
We could barely see the players
From our faraway bleacher seats.
What *did* matter was that
We were with our friends,
Laughing, joking, screaming,
Breathing beer-scented air
On a schoolday in May.
Welcome guests in the home of
Whitey and Yogi, Mickey and Roger.

The Fleet Four-Year-Old

With breath-taking speed, she
Moves from tears to laughter;
Wrecks newly-cleaned rooms;
Learns off-color expressions;
Makes best friends and worst enemies;
Masters multi-verse silly songs;
Shifts from tantrum to sound discourse;
Forgives her parents' indiscretions;
Grows up.

Spare Time

She bakes, he writes.
Her breads, his poems
Are simple, basic, without
Affectation or flourish.
Created as gifts for
Families by birth, for
Families by choice.
Means of reaching out,
Connecting, sharing,
Nurturing.

Senryu

stunned fiancé—
her gown's price tag
has a comma

·

post-miscarriage,
trying to return
Baby Names book

·

going blind
she tries to memorize
grandchildren's faces

·

after the divorce
heart-shaped birthmark
becomes cancerous

·

tries to impress her:
places their order in French
with the busboy

·

at dawn—old couple
scours a parking lot
searching for change

·

restaurant hostess ...
a manicured fingernail
digging in her ear

Senryu

public library ...
child searches under "C"
for coloring books

.

in his prison cell—
a dog-eared volume of
pastoral haiku

.

longtime couple
consuming 4-course dinner
wordlessly

.

winter street corner—
stiletto heels
grinding the ice

.

faculty party ...
linguist speaking gibberish
to colleague's baby

.

wraps her fingers
around the baby's chest
absorbing heartbeats

.

city girl ...
watering the grass
in a sidewalk's crack

Alone

As a child in the city
He would dream:
Coming home from school,
All apartment houses on his block
Became precisely the same—
No numbers on buildings,
No letters on doors,
No names on mailboxes.
He couldn't remember
What floor he lived on.
To find his parents,
Every door in every building
Had to be knocked,
Every occupant, disturbed.
He would awaken
Before finding his home,
Crying, terrified.

Thirty years later,
The dream returns—
Not in his sleep,
But when he enters
His child's bedroom
To hold and comfort
In the middle of the night.

Phallic Stage Follies

At four,
Legos are shaped into guns,
Popsicle sticks into swords,
Twigs into rifles.
Last night,
Holding a hand-made weapon,
Growls at his father,
"Say yaw pwayyuhs!"
Son, dead serious, views
Himself as Clint Eastwood.
Father, hysterical, sees
A pint-sized Elmer Fudd.

With her Therapist

She'll curse, rage, weep. Share
Intimate memories, fears, fantasies.
Reveal dark, petty, infantile shades.
But she won't bare all without
Earrings, lipstick, contact lenses.

Age/Gender/Temperament

The emergency room doctor
Proclaims, pneumonia, so
She goes home alone to
Pack him a bag and
Inform their children.
She enters the house
Armed with pastries.
The 7-year-old girl
Immediately, fearfully asks
Where's Daddy?
Mom, matter-of-factly,
Lays out the sweets, responds
He needs to stay a few ...
Daughter interrupts,
Sobbing hysterically.
Three-year-old son
Ponders it all quietly, asks
Can I have another doughnut?

Rejection Notice

But one word: *Sorry.*
Editor's condolence or
Poem's quality?

Dinner Guest

Daughters shoot glances—
Curious, hurt, angry—
At her latest flame
Sitting uncomfortably,
Unknowingly
At the head of the table
In their father's place.

States of the Game

Looks at Michigan,
sees a catcher's mitt.
At Colorado and Wyoming,
first and second base.
Nevada, home plate.
Tennessee, base path.
Florida, broken bat.
(Delaware and New Jersey,
slivers of that bat.)
Baseball fever rages
in geography class.

Eyes of the Beholder

The 4-year-old
Is fitted for glasses.
Mother and father fret
He's too young,
He'll be laughed at,
He's physically imperfect—
What else may be wrong?
Older sister, 8,
Adopted, Korean-born
Like her brother, cries
We no longer look the same,
His eyes aren't like mine,
I'm alone.
The 4-year-old
Examines self in mirror,
Smiles, concludes, "Cool!"

Best Defense

With twins, parents can
Play kids *man-to-man;*
But, with four, they moan
And must switch to *zone.*

50 Years after Auschwitz

At night,
Alone, in his chair,
What did he see when
Staring out the window?
His mother's face—
Warm, serene
Or pale, gaunt?
Friday night dinner—
Boiled beef and horseradish
Or thin, rancid broth?
Smoke—
Coming from his father's pipe
Or from the crematoria?
To protect us, he never shared.
To spare him, we never asked.

Rosh Hashanah

Learning is rebirth.
Start of school, Jewish new year
Coincide each Fall.

Reflections of an Adoptive Parent

Family nights at their schools
always evoke flashes of sadness.
Red-haired, freckle-faced mothers
and daughters,
Chiseled-chinned fathers with
like-jawed sons
Chat, play, fight, sit together.
I look at them, then at my children
both of Korean parents.
My love and delight in them is
immeasurably deep, yet at these times
I long for superficial similarities.
I wish they possessed
my cheekbones, my wife's blue eyes,
a shared genetic lineage,
a biological/constitutional connection,
my father's smile.

Two-Year-Old Artist

She holds her crayons
Like tiny tubes of toothpaste,
Squeezing out colors.

Haiku/Senryu

last child moves out—
mother removes leaf from
her kitchen table

•

homeless man
sips cold night's coffee—
black, snow-dusted

•

rope hammock
and a spider's web
swaying in rhythm

•

summer heat, drought
take their toll—
hunchbacked sunflower

•

pigeons preening
in a rainbow,
becoming pheasants

•

lonely five-year-old
turns off the TV,
dials 9-1-1

•

elderly man
looks both ways
then crosses the room

Haiku/Senryu

Christian photographer
prompts Jewish bride:
Smile, Jesus loves you

.

overweight trucker
self-advertises:
Wide Load

.

busy phone lines
on January 2nd—
fitness center

.

bored teenager ...
gluing pennies
to city sidewalks

.

casting their lines ...
poet, fisherman
hope to connect

.

two blinking stars,
a Cheshire cat moon—
April Fool's night

.

Auschwitz survivor
stares at grandson's arm:
skull-and-bones tattoo

Senryu

six-year-old
with a stale French bread
reinvents baseball

.

pajamas with feet ...
youngest child's last pair
valued more than gold

.

match point ...
server's mother
covers her eyes

.

eight months after
losing her child, fearing
May's second Sunday

.

fifth-grade graduates ...
blossoming girls,
stick-figured boys

.

day camp counselors
whispering lullabies ...
the first overnight

.

"She looks just like you"—
adoptive parents
can't help but smile

Champion

Each day provides
Seventeen sleepless hours,
Each hour, a boxing round.
Depression, the opponent.
Jabs hopelessness, dejection.
Absorbs counterpunches of doubt,
Uppercuts suicidal ideation.
Withstands daily punishment,
Both self- and other-inflicted.
Yet refuses to retire
From the ring.

Birth Father, Birth Mother

She never asks about him.
It's always her—
How old was she?
What did she look like?
Why did she give me up?
Did she ever hold me?
His absence barely registers.
Hers continues to puzzle
And wound.

For Alexandra

Paraplegics waltzing
Obsessives relaxing
Lepers rejoicing
The mute singing
The blind painting
Schizophrenics connecting
Stillborns thriving.
Heaven.

Rest Stop

New Jersey Turnpike men's room.
Three-year-old boy drops his pants,
Walks over to children's urinal
And goes to work.
To his right stand six
Leather-and-chain clad
Motorcyclists, similarly engaged.
Father of boy observes
The magnificent seven from behind
And longs for a camera.

Six-Year-Old's Avalanche

She pulled the cord, out it poured;
I couldn't believe what she'd stored:
Six pencils, all broken,
An amusement park token.
Wrappers of gum and candy,
A photograph of Brandy.
A quarter, four pennies,
A coupon from *Denny's*.
One fuzz-covered lemon drop,
A badly fractured lollipop.
Keys, clips, tissues, a brush,
Candy bars reduced to mush.
Assorted papers, caramel vapors.
Maybe it wouldn't be such a bad idea
To empty her bag more than once a year.

Poetic Progression

Editor's rejection,
Author's dejection,
Greater reflection,
Substantial correction,
Approaches perfection.

Jobs

Over the summer, lost
Her father to cancer.
First day of seventh grade,
Handed a form asking
About parents' occupations.
Next to mother, writes Secretary.
Next to father, Watching over me.

Wyoming

A store marquee proclaiming
"Guns, Ammo, Chain Saws,"
A Country-Western version
of "Under the Boardwalk"
on the radio,
A "Pony Expresso" cappuccino
drive-through on Main Street,
Greet and bewilder
the Easterners on vacation.

The New Member

Staring at their baby sister
They worry.
Aged 7 and 4.
Adopted as infants.
They understand that the baby
Is their parents' only birth child.
The eldest verbalizes the fear:
Mom and Dad won't love her as much.
She wasn't chosen like we were.

Neologisms

As precious as toothless smiles,
Finger-painted masterpieces, and
Unsolicited kisses are children's
Verbal works of art:
I blessed youed (for I sneezed);
Porkies (porcupine quills);
Father Cereal (the *Quaker Oats* man);
Bookshelves in the head (book-smart).
Creations as wonderful as rainbows
And, sadly, as short-lived.

Senryu

in their cars
screaming parents
await "Happy Meals"

.

at the library
a homeless woman
browses an atlas

.

over croissants
and cappuccino, reading
about Kosovo

.

failing eyes
cannot detect
her son's graying hair

.

spring cleaning—
he featherdusts
his self-help books

.

Alzheimer parents
now, nursing home roommates—
together, alone

.

the blind scholar
rolls up his sleeves,
begins to read

Senryu

manic-depressive
on lithium
misses the edges

.

inner-city child
observes alliteration:
Lou's Liquors, Bail Bonds

.

widowed young mother
eavesdrops on an old couple
in mid-argument

.

hyperactive child
in Grand Central Station
blending unnoticed

.

at the checkout
old man sees a young beauty,
hides the bran flakes

.

full body checking
in suits, evening gowns ...
wedding smorgasbord

.

roadside diner ...
his five-year-old downing
shots of half-and-half

Haiku/Senryu

on the porch
angry blue jay pecks
an Orioles cap

.

fireman's lecture ...
bored first graders
stare at his ax

.

sixtieth birthday ...
grandfather buys himself
diamond earring

.

college reunion ...
still bragging about
his G.P.A.

.

plastic slipcovers
adorning broken chairs ...
Grandma's living room

.

mother of five
purchasing diapers
for her father

.

through the slits
of an old trailer ...
a cow's sad eyes

David and David

"Bringed,"
"For him and I,"
"The men what went,"
Catastrophe pronounced "cat-is-truff" …
The six-year-old's errors of spelling,
Grammar, pronunciation, usage
Echo those made by
The Polish-born grandfather
He never had a chance to meet.

Dawn

Analytic functions, French infinitives.
Chemical formulas, Freudian theories.
Regression equations, factorial designs.
Names, dates, algorithms, laws,
Hypotheses, principles, proofs.
All absorbed by the college
Cleaning crew.

Six-Year-Old Theologian

Uncommonly solemn
Sadly concludes
There's one thing
God cannot do—
Have a birthday party.

Brothers

Mother died, and they came
To divide the estate.
A coin flip would determine
Who chose first.
Knowing his brother as he did,
Knowing his love of family,
Of music, of tradition,
The younger knew the elder would choose
The photograph of Father
Cradling his cherished violin.

The coin was tossed, the younger won.
The photo! The photo! he cried.
Thank goodness, sighed the elder.
I was afraid you'd select
The big-screen television.

Family Balance

Happy in their marriage,
Fulfilled in their careers,
Their siblings show them
No anger, no envy
Provided they remain
Childless.

Progress

At 15, I would dream of being
In an unfamiliar classroom,
Facing an unexpected final
In an unknown subject.

At 25, of standing
In a cavernous lecture hall,
Addressing my esteemed professors,
Naked, except for my socks.

At 35, of having
My Ph.D. wrested from me
For lack of one college credit
In volleyball.

Perhaps, by 50,
Struggling, wakeful feelings of
Competence, genuineness, security
Will begin to put such dreams
To merciful rest.

Death Valley

In front of a general store
They slouch on a bench,
Dressed in cowboy hats, boots,
Denim work shirts, bandannas.
One plays *My Darling Clementine*
Softly on an old harmonica
While the others tap in time
With their boots and spurs....
Three German tourists.

Life Shavers

They don't end or cripple it,
Just tear it, wear it down.
Children's whining, old-age aches;
Stubborn splinters, mysterious rashes;
Missed trains, jammed staplers;
Shoddy toys, cheap sentiment;
Ethnic jokes, undeserved honors.
Imperceptibly, relentlessly
Peel off seconds of life.

Three-Year-Old

Daughter of two psychologists,
Witnesses them arguing.
Screams at each,
"What's your issue?"
Parents, terrified,
Anticipate adolescence.

Weak Wattage

Pundits of the left,
Sages of the right,
Invariably transmit
More heat than light.

Reach Out, Touch No One

You got e-mail? Cool!
We can communicate each day.

Yes. But I remind you
My desk is thirty feet away!

A Traditional Rosh Hashanah

Guilt-ridden, her parents
Wait for her to return.
Non-observers, they allowed her
To go with a friend to
High Holiday services
(Followed by lunch with
The friend's grandmother).
They silently chide themselves:
We should be more observant.
We shouldn't rely on others to
Give her a religious education.
The daughter returns and is
Peppered with questions.
How were services?
—Boring.
What was the sermon about?
—I wasn't listening.
Was lunch at the grandmother's fun?
—We didn't eat at her house
(Picked her up and ate out).
Where did you go?
—*Taco Bell.*

Laura and Erica

They are introduced.
A 10-year-old,
An 11-month-old
Born of, adopted by
Eight different parents.
Americans by way of Korea.
Eyes meet, smiles follow.
New connections made,
Old connections re-established.
Each has found a sister.

December Nights

Ivory white, pearl white
Gray/white, green/white
Brown/white, black/white
Half-white, eighth-white
Speck-white, all-white.
So many pieces, so little difference.
Half-mad, nearly snow-blind
He presses on
Determined to complete
The gift from his children:
"Winter Woods" jigsaw puzzle.

Adopted Child

A classmate moves away,
A friend stops calling,
An uncle dies,
A school year ends,
A neighbor divorces.
Every loss a cut and sear
Echoing her birthmother's good-bye.

7 Going on 8

Small, subtle, spirit-lifting are
The pleasures she provides:
Offering a heartfelt, unsolicited
Thank you.
Saying "brought" rather than
"Brang" or "bringed."
Letting her little brother
Have the bigger piece.
Asking to visit the library
On a sunny day.
Not looking mortified when
Kissed by her father.

Haiku/Senryu

senior prom night—
strapless gown laid out on bed
next to teddy bears

.

grandfather's eyebrows—
untrimmed gray hedges protect
two blue irises

.

windblown plastic bags
adorn inner-city tree—
winter foliage

.

thin rainbow candles
aglow in December cold ...
Hanukkah sundowns

.

post-stroke,
tears forming
as words fail

.

newly-divorced
fifty-five, bitter—
irons his first shirt

.

midday, asleep
soft breezes blow in her crib—
baby exhales

Senryu

father of twin boys
feebly setting limits:
I mean it this time

•

graduation day—
under their robes,
T-shirts and tattoos

•

salesman's wife
on tenth anniversary—
dines alone

•

sensible shoes,
multi-pierced ears—
first grade teacher

•

latest haiku
evokes same response:
Is this all?

•

summertime camping—
city sophisticate
samples fish jerky

•

Christmas tradition ...
Jewish family dines
with chopsticks

Priorities

How's your year been?
I asked the noted scholar.
Perfect! Simply perfect!
Was his elated response.
(How, I thought, could
One's year be perfect if
One's planet contained
Bosnia, Rwanda, Somalia,
A flood-ravaged heartland,
Children with handguns,
Neighbors without homes?)
What made it so perfect?
—I received a huge grant.
To study what?
—Narcissism.
Perfect.

Lionhearted

Amidst a forest of legs
[Table, chair, and human],
The intrepid toddler lurches,
Caroming off hard bodies
Like a multi-limbed pinball.
Falling, rising, falling, rising,
A courageous, undaunted explorer
Seeking adventure and knowledge
In a land of giants.

Anti-Depressant

The tip is rounded,
The serration is removed,
Yet the knife still wounds.

Greatest Gifts

Freedom and toddlers
Exact the same noble price:
Ceaseless vigilance.

Businessman

Dying, he kisses
Tearful wife, sons. Gently says,
Clean out the vault, then mourn.

Four-Year-Olds at Work

Two children, one glass.
In the absence of sharing,
Two full-bodied whines.

First Halloween

At two, dressed as a Dalmatian,
He knocks and rings, and
When doors open, marches
Directly into strangers' kitchens
Looking for treasures.

Late in the evening, he
Spies a cat, madly takes off.
Poor bewildered cat—
Being chased by 2-legged dog
In turn pursued by exhausted
Father with flashlight.

Unaware

The one-year-old, so
Busy crying, longing,
Forgets that he is holding
The wish-fulfilling treat
In his clenched fist.

So, too, the adult,
Preoccupied with what
He does not have
At home, at work,
Remains oblivious
To his hidden treasures.

On the Road to Socialization

When approaching a stranger,
Particularly a young one,
He would reach out and,
Without anger or ill will,
Grab a nose, jab an eye, or
Smack a forehead.
Simply, his nine-month-old way
Of saying, Hello. I'm David.
I want to understand you.
After a year of mentoring by
Mother, father, and elder sister,
He now greets/strokes unfamiliar faces
Ardently, yet softly, sweetly, while
Whispering words he's heard
Countless times:
Gentle, gentle.

Yankee Stadium

A Bronx oasis.
A pin-striped Mount Olympus
For hero-starved boys.

Senryu

baseball fan ...
mustard and beer adorn
her new tanktop

.

astronomy class—
bracing for wisecracks
he says "Uranus"

.

evening news ...
anchorman smiles
between tragedies

.

career day ...
pilot, ornithologist
wait in the wings

.

at cliff's edge
he tries to decide:
spit or jump

.

board meeting ...
elderly chairman
breaks into song

.

talent show ...
six-year-old soprano
sings *Ol' Man River*

Senryu

sunshine breaks through
after a week of darkness ...
in-laws board the plane

.

approaching the bar
trying to remove
his wedding ring

.

elderly waiter
recites the specials ...
served two weeks ago

.

Nobel winner's death
overshadowed by
movie star's arrest

.

all night
she stays awake
counting heartbeats

.

fourth-grade cellist
keeping time
with both feet

.

next morning ...
bride's father finds rice
in his wallet

Senryu

blind woman's home—
clocks and computers speak
in many voices

.

taxidermist's sign:
"We Buy All Horns" ...
man brings bugle

.

rainy summer night ...
gray-haired man playing poker
with green-haired grandson

.

their car hits a deer ...
she strokes its face,
he takes its picture

.

satellite dishes
beside the reservation's
run-down homes

.

asked how it's going ...
stoic, cancer-ridden boy
sighs, "Could be worse"

.

old fans reminisce ...
ten-cent franks, legal spitballs
all-white teams

Haiku/Senryu

calorie-conscious
girlfriends, order dessert:
one eclair, four forks

.

three-year-old's ears ...
ER doctor performs
raisinectomy

.

at the pharmacy ...
principal sees two students,
ditches the condoms

.

girlfriend's parents
can't see beyond
his Asian eyes

.

trees on fire
shed their flames
in an autumn wind

.

grade-school trombonist—
harmonizing while
poking the flutists

.

hand-me-down shirt
decorated with
three brothers' stains

Senryu

murderer's neighbors
describe him as polite,
his lawn as well-kept

.

TV interview
of three *Valley Girls* …
subtitles needed

.

debutante walks in
on the Stein Bar Mitzvah …
wrong banquet hall

.

estranged mother
finds out from a friend
her daughter gave birth

.

in the OR …
brain surgeon tries to recall
Opie's last name

.

the five-year-old cries
as Dad does the eulogy …
turtle funeral

.

wolf-whistler
realizing too late
it is his sister

Senryu

bathroom mirror—
their teenage son
works on his scowl

·

bus station diner—
a homeless woman
insists on decaf

·

child at Christmas-time
unsure what to wish for:
world peace or new skates

·

dirt-filled popgun
discharges in toddler's eyes ...
father licks them clean

·

longing to be touched
the elderly widow gets
her first pedicure

·

multiple cuts ...
arguing with his children
while shaving

·

ten-year-old's wallet ...
one dollar bill
and eighteen photos

Senryu

shopping for his wife
forty-year-old man
buys his first tampons

·

father, teenager
sit down for a talk ...
shrugs outnumber words

·

wedding night ...
fifty-year-old virgin
says a prayer

·

luxury health spa
overrun with accountants
on April sixteenth

·

college freshman
asleep in class
dreams he's taking notes

·

keeps on playing
through pain, with pluck—
arthritic harpist

·

Easter Sunday ...
grandfather can't recall
where he hid the eggs

Senryu

his wife,
reading a romance novel
at the ballgame

·

highly anxious child,
unorthodox therapist
meet at *McDonald's*

·

three televisions
in a family's home ...
the same program

·

on her back, awake ...
a tiny pool of tears
in each ear

·

his four-year-old
trying to keep *Jell-O* still
with tape and thumbtacks

·

pubescent daughter
setting new records
for eye rolls, door slams

·

his name above hers
forty years after his death
on each check she writes

Senryu

the hour gets late ...
candles, toddler
are melting down

•

wife observes him
staring at their daughter
in a short, tight dress

•

interfaith household ...
matzo crumbs, jelly beans
between the cushions

•

Saturday morning ...
an exercise bicycle
at each garage sale

•

their long blond hair
in matching ponytails ...
father and daughter

•

math professor
hears from the bank—
overdrawn again

•

a country drive—
the loud mooing
of my children

Katie

Our five-year-olds were happily
    playing cards.
Katie can read, exulted her mother.
Katie, come here.
Katie, come *here*!
Katie, read this headline.
Katie complied, perfectly yet joylessly,
Then quickly returned to my daughter
And resumed laughing.

Katie's really special, I remarked later.
She sure is, beamed my daughter.
She can shuffle!

What Became of John?

Jackson, Tyler, Taylor, Carter—
Last names of four ex-Presidents;
And, now, trendy first names of
Nursery school residents.

Old-World Father

Bewildered by our
Watching televised athletes.
Play yourself ... or read!

Freshman

Came for advisement.
Missing six fingers,
Three from each hand.
Left wrist bore a grid of
Short, razor-thin scars.
Eyes, unable to make contact,
Danced wildly about the room.
Fragile, frightened, damaged,
Appeared a victim of abuse
(Both self- and other-inflicted).
First words:
Tell me what to take,
I want to help people.

Lethal

Minutes past curfew,
Scorches home doing eighty
In Dad's car. Scared, drunk.

34th Street

Young Puerto Rican woman,
With backpack and shopping bags,
Pushes her baby in a carriage
Through the subway doors
On to the platform.
She shuffles to the long staircase
Leading up to the street.
A Black man, unknown to her,
Approaches and, without saying a word,
Grabs the front of the carriage.
The mother, holding its handle, and
The man, looking straight ahead,
Carry the baby up the stairs.
Once at the top,
He sets the carriage down and walks away,
Not looking behind as the mother shouts
"Thank you" to the back of his head.

Getting It

To be content, I must create.
A work of art, of literature, of science;
Something unique, something my own.
And to be happy, truly happy,
My creation must be recognized,
Acclaimed, and enduring.

How sad, his wife replied,
That evoking a smile, teaching a lesson,
Watching a sunset, relieving a burden
Provide you with neither contentment
Nor happiness.

You don't get it, he shouted.
Thank goodness, she sighed.

Index of Original Sources

Many of the poems presented in this volume have been published elsewhere. Listed below are the titles of these poems and the journals, newspapers, periodicals, and books in which they first appeared.

In **The Wall Street Journal:** *Perfectionist; Name Calling; Weak Wattage*

In **Fauquier Poetry Journal:** *Wedding Dance; Street Scene; Three-Year-Old Author; Better Living Through Science; Corner Store, 1966; Loan; Rejection Notice; Eyes of the Beholder; Death Valley; Three-Year-Old; 34th Street*

In **The Baltimore Sun:** *Line Art; 77290; Thankless*

In **The Baltimore Evening Sun:** *Lessons; Entitlement; A Mother's Gift; Wonderland; Toddlersaurus; Balance; Father and Son; Valentines; First Day of Kindergarten; Semantic Shifts; Blessed; City Playground; In Hiding; Passover Seder; Priorities; Greatest Gifts; Businessman; Four-Year-Olds at Work; Progress; Old-World Father; Lethal*

In **Journal of Poetry Therapy:** *Halloween at Children's Hospital; Survivor; Champion*

In **Muse of Fire:** *high school commencement; in her garage; Best Defense; 50 Years after Auschwitz; pigeons preening; lonely five-year-old; elderly man; Christian photographer; Poetic Progression; Jobs; Neologisms; Six-Year-Old's Avalanche; in their cars; at the library; over croissants; failing eyes; inner-city child; widowed young mother; hyperactive child; at the checkout;*

*Life Shavers; Reach Out, Touch No One; A Traditional Rosh
Hashanah; December Nights; Adopted Child; baseball fan; evening
news; career day; at cliff's edge; board meeting; talent show;
sunshine breaks through; approaching the bar; elderly waiter;
Nobel winner's death; taxidermist's sign; rainy summer night;
their car hits a deer; satellite dishes; asked how it's going; old fans
reminisce; calorie-conscious; three-year-old's ears; at the pharmacy;
girlfriend's parents; trees on fire; murderer's neighbors; TV
interview; estranged mother; in the OR; the five-year-old cries;
dirt-filled popgun; longing to be touched; multiple cuts;
ten-year-old's wallet; shopping for his wife; father, teenager;
wedding night; luxury health spa; college freshman; Easter
Sunday; highly anxious child; on her back, awake; his
four-year-old; pubescent daughter; his name above hers; the hour
gets late; wife observes him; Freshman*

In **Modern Haiku**: *high noon—buzzards; goes to the market;
pointing, laughing; old Southern lady; faculty party; post-stroke;
graduation day; astronomy class; wolf-whistler; bathroom mirror;
their long blond hair*

In **black bough**: *ankle bracelet; sensible shoes*

In **Haiku Headlines**: *beach chair on front porch; centenarian;
eight-year-old's boyfriend; tortilla chip; stunned fiancé; tries to
impress her; restaurant hostess; last child moves out; homeless man;
rope hammock; busy phone lines; two blinking stars; Auschwitz
survivor; senior prom night; thin rainbow candles; debutante walks
in; his wife; three televisions*

In **The Pegasus Review**: *casting their lines; Urban Escapist;
Disconnected; The Fleet Four-Year-Old; public library; in his
prison cell; States of the Game; summer heat; The New Member;
newly-divorced; latest haiku; First Halloween; child at
Christmas-time*

In **Welcome Home**: *Special Delivery from Korea; Second Born; side-by-side, carpooled; Spare Time; Two-Year-Old Artist; Birth Father, Birth Mother; midday, asleep; father of twin boys; On the Road to Socialization; Katie; Unaware; Getting It*

In **Timber Creek Review**: *Empathy; Therapy; Saturdays; Glory Days in the Bronx; Age/Gender/Temperament; Family Balance; Wyoming; Brothers; Yankee Stadium; What Became of John?*

In **Network News: A Quarterly Publication of Adoptive Family Network**: *In the Waiting Room; Behind a Six-toothed Smile; At the Market; Answers for the Novice; Encores; Juggler; Laura and Erica; 7 Going on 8*

In **Night Roses**: *A Toddler's Night's Sleep; February/June*

In **Heartbeat**: *Laura, at 6*

In **The Pearl**: *Too Long in Academia*

In **Jewish Spectator**: *Survivor's Handball; Eraser*

In **Endless Skies of Blue (D. Zeiger, ed.)**: *Bertha*

In **The Villager**: *Kindergarten Graduation; Mornings; longtime couple; grandfather's eyebrows; windblown plastic bags; Lionhearted*

In **Piedmont Literary Review**: *stalemate*

In **Frogpond**: *in mourning; salesman's wife; a country drive*

In **Jewish Communication Network: Verses of Judaism (On line)**: *Bedtime Questions; Rosh Hashanah*

In **Up Dare?**: *post-miscarriage; going blind; after the divorce; at dawn—old couple; For Alexandra; spring cleaning; Alzheimer parents; the blind scholar; manic-depressive; all night; blind woman's home; bus station diner; keeps on playing*

In **Words of Wisdom:** *winter street corner; Alone; Phallic Stage Follies; Reflections of an Adoptive Parent; overweight trucker; Rest Stop*

In **Voices: The Art and Science of Psychotherapy:** *With her Therapist*

In **Mediphors: A Literary Journal of the Health Professions:** *Anti-Depressant*

In **Tundra:** *Saturday morning*

Author's Note

Robert H. Deluty was born and raised in New York City and currently lives in Ellicott City, Maryland with his wife, Barbara, and their children, Laura and David. He received his Ph.D. in Clinical-Community Psychology from the State University of New York at Buffalo. Since 1980, he has been a psychology professor at the University of Maryland, Baltimore County.